COPPARD, Yvonne

Abuse

The moral right of the author has been asserted in accordance with the Copyright,
Designs and Patents Act 1988

Acknowledgments

Many thanks to the following organisations for their kind permission to use copyright material in this book:

Childline, for quotes from children

The European Campaign to Raise Awareness of Violence Against Women, for domestic violence posters

The Daily Telegraph, for the following articles:
'Mother left her baby . . .' by Nigel Bunyan
'Mother faces jail for killing son . . .' by Sue Clough

National ... ... :H's Net
Smart ru ...

Dedication

This book is dedicated to everyone who wants to do their bit to try and make child abuse something that used to happen. That includes me and, if you're reading this book, it includes you, too.

A Word About Words

What's a child, or 'young person'? Baby, infant, junior, pre-teen, adolescent or teenager? Mostly, I've used the legal definition of a child, which means anyone under the age of 18. Apologies to anyone who feels this is the wrong choice for someone of their particular age.

What do you do when you want to say something that applies equally to males and females? Frequent use of 'he or she' is clumsy, and 's/he' doesn't feel right either, so I've gone for 'they' or 'you', even though it's not good grammar and will drive your English teachers up the wall.

Finally, what is a parent? When I use the word, I mean the person or people with the main responsibility for looking after the child, so it can include step-parents, foster parents, and live-in partners of parents, foster carers and relatives who've taken over the care of the child.

Contents

We Haven't Always Had Child Abuse . . .

. . . at least, that's what people used to think. In olden days, children were simply possessions of their parents. No-one would dream of questioning a parent's explanation of what had happened to their own child. There was no such thing as a physically abused child, only a very 'clumsy' one who kept having accidents or a very 'naughty' one who needed to be punished.

In 1866, in the United States of America, the American Society for the Prevention of Cruelty to Animals (the ASPCA) was formed, but there was no such society for children. Then, five years after the Society was started, an interesting case reached the news.

A little girl was being beaten every day by her stepmother, and people who knew about it wanted to protect her. But the stepmother was not breaking the law, and it looked as though there was nothing that could be done. In despair and frustration, the people trying to protect the child turned to the ASPCA.

The ASPCA took the case to court, and managed to prove that the term 'animal' could include a child. The little girl was saved from more abuse – and suddenly the general public woke up to the fact that there was no law against this sort of behaviour. There was outrage that the law did more to protect animals than it did children. So in 1871, five years after the ASPCA was started to protect animals, the Society for the Protection of Children was formed.

For the first time, people started to say that it was not entirely a parent's business what happened to a child. People started to accept that some injuries and even deaths of children were because their parents were ill-treating them. From that came an agreement that neglected and beaten children should be protected from their families.

A few years later, things started happening in the United Kingdom, too. The Reverend Benjamin Waugh was working as a priest in the slums of London, and he was shocked by the way many children were treated. He was determined to help the plight of children he saw being regularly abused and neglected. At that time, parents had absolute rights over their children unless they actually killed them. Any other type of cruelty was within the law. Just as in the United States, there was a law to protect animals, but not children.

The Reverend Waugh changed that with the formation of the London Society for the Prevention of Cruelty to Children, in 1884. Five years later, it became the National Society for the Prevention of Cruelty to Children, with Queen Victoria as its Royal Patron. This is the famous NSPCC we still have today. In those days inspectors patrolled the streets of London by bicycle, collecting vulnerable and ill-treated children and taking them to safety. These days there are telephone help lines, computer sites, drop-in centres and thousands of different projects going on every day across the country.

Even with the work of the NSPCC, it wasn't until the 1960s that Dr Henry Kempe introduced the term 'battered baby syndrome'. He did it to shock people into taking more seriously what he had been saying for years – that physical injuries on children were not always accidental. Sometimes, parents were deliberately harming or neglecting them.

In the 1970s people who were working with physically abused and neglected children began also to identify another kind of abuse. Some children were damaged, not by neglect or physical abuse, but by emotional bullying: constant humiliation or rejection, or terrifying a child.

Child sexual abuse was the last type of abuse to be properly recognised, in the 1980s. This is the most secret and silent of abuses; it does not usually leave physical clues, as neglect or physical abuse might. People who work in child protection often say that sexual abuse is the most difficult abuse to deal with – but as our understanding grows, so does our knowledge of what to do about it.

Today, child protection is an essential part of the job for everyone who works with children – teachers, dinner ladies, social workers, doctors and nurses, police, childminders, youth workers – you name it, if it's a job that involves being with children, child protection will be on everyone's mind.

What Child Abuse Is . . . And What It Isn't

The definitions of child abuse in this book are based on a law called The Children Act 1989, which gave birth to most of the policies and procedures that child protection workers have to follow today.

In law you are a child from the day you are born until your 18th birthday. Even though you can legally consent to sex at age 16, child protection procedures can protect you from sexual abuse in the family for another two years after that. In very rare circumstances the child protection system can even protect an unborn baby by saying what must happen as soon as the baby is born e.g. it is not to be left alone with the parent.

Child abuse happens when someone who is connected by family to the child deliberately causes them harm. This person could be a parent or relative, step parent, family friend, someone who regularly babysits the child, and so on – anyone who has a close connection to the family, whether or not they are blood relatives.

One thing that abuse is not is an attack from a stranger. If a child is attacked and hurt by a stranger while out playing, for instance, it is not usually a child protection case. It is still a crime, of course, but it is one that the police will deal with in a different way to child abuse. They do not need to worry about whether the child will be safe at home with their family. Unless, that is, the child was out playing very late, or in a dangerous place, or there is some other reason to suspect that the family are not taking proper care of the child.

So, child abuse happens when someone who is supposed to be caring for the child turns on, and damages, the child in some way.

The term used by the law for this is 'significant harm'.

If a social worker and/or a police officer is told about a child by someone who is concerned about the child's safety, this concept of significant harm has to guide their thinking. Crossing the border from 'not the best way to bring a child up' or 'could be heading for trouble' to 'this child is actually in danger of being seriously hurt if we don't do something' is what makes a child protection case, rather than a case where a child is in need of some help, but not actually in danger from their own parents. Where that border is crossed is where 'significant harm' lies.

If significant harm has happened to the child – or if it seems likely it might happen – there will be a discussion usually involving social workers, police and other people who work with children such as teachers, nurses and so on. What happens at this meeting is covered later in this book, in the chapter called 'Child Protection Conferences'.

When people talk about abuse, they usually divide it into four different categories.
        Neglect
        Physical Abuse
        Sexual Abuse
        Emotional Abuse

In the following chapters we will look at what we mean by all these terms. We will also look at how abuse can happen and what you can do about it, whether it is you or someone you know that is at risk. There will also be information about some of the other things that can go wrong in families and put children at risk of being harmed, such as: domestic violence; alcohol-dependent parents; drug-dependent parents; parents with mental illness and racial abuse in the family.

At the end of the book is a list of websites and telephone numbers that will help you find out more. Keep them handy in case you – or a friend – ever need to use them.

Neglect

Two young brothers in North Wales, aged four and one years old, developed a disease called marasmus that is usually only seen in starving children in places like Africa. Marasmus is a wasting disease, which causes wrinkles and sores all over the skin. The four-year-old could not sit up without help, and the one-year-old was too weak to eat.

The boys are now happy with foster parents. Their mother, who wore designer clothes even though her children were starving, was jailed for 15 months.

Neglect is not usually about what parents or carers *do*; it is mostly about things that they *don't* do. In order to grow and develop, right from tiny babies to (hopefully) strapping, healthy young adults, we all need certain things.

- We need food – not just any old food, but the right kind of food in the right quantities to help our bodies grow and develop properly.
- We need shelter – somewhere that's home, where we can escape from the winter cold or the burning sun or the pelting rain.
- We need clothing and shoes to keep us warm and protected in winter. In summer, we need clothes (or creams) that will protect our skin from burning.
- As tiny children, we need at least one adult who will protect us from harm – someone who will make sure dangerous chemicals and medicines are locked away; who will stop us getting out onto busy roads; who will teach us how to play safely and make sure we don't get into danger.
- We need to be taken care of when we get sick, especially when we are too small to seek medical help for ourselves. We need to have someone who will take us to the doctor or the hospital when it becomes necessary.

○ Just as importantly as all the things listed above, we need physical and emotional affection – we need to be held, and hugged, smiled at, and cooed over, especially as babies and young children. (Even when it gets embarrassing to be fussed over, when we reach our teens, we need to know that there is someone at home who *wants* to fuss!)

The last point is an interesting one because we often think about neglect as though it's all to do with physical things. But if you give a baby everything they need physically – all the right food, clothing and so on – it will not be enough. If there is no stimulation from adult company, no hugs and smiles and chatter, a tiny baby will not thrive. Put simply, the baby won't grow, won't learn to talk, won't be able to function properly as they get older.

If a child does not get any affection from parents, this is a neglect of the child's needs. But it is also a kind of emotional abuse. As we shall see later, neglect and emotional abuse have quite a lot of crossover with each other.

What it is and what it isn't

Every family goes through bad patches sometimes, and this can cause problems for the children. Maybe for a while the adults are too busy with their own troubles to take much notice of their children. The marriage might be breaking up, for example, or someone might have a serious illness. There could be a new baby taking up lots of time, or problems like losing jobs or having to move house, or someone dying. All these things put a lot of stress on a family, and for a few days the children might not be very well looked after.

This is not necessarily neglect. Hopefully, after the initial shock, or with a bit of help from a friend, relative or neighbour, things will get better and the children will be well looked after again. Neglect is something that goes on for such a long time that the child's health or growth or development suffers. In the words of the Children Act, neglect is 'the *persistent* failure to meet a child's basic physical and/or psychological needs, likely to result in the *serious impairment* of the child's health or development.'

So neglect is something that can go on for a long time before the Social Services or other agencies that work with children step in. Of course, if a baby or a very young child is being neglected, the effects on the child's body will be seen much sooner. Babies can become ill very quickly if they are not fed, changed or kept warm. In the case of a baby or tiny child, neglect would have to be acted upon much more quickly than with, say, an older child who would be able to go and ask a neighbour for food, or steal some. There's also a good chance that the problem will be noticed by a teacher if the child is old enough to be in school.

How neglect happens

How do people learn to be parents? Not usually at school, and not usually from books either. Very few parents take classes in how to bring up a child. They are just expected to know how to do it. But what if you don't? What if your own parents were violent or cruel or not willing to put much effort into raising you? What if you grew up in care, or your parent was drugged out or seriously mentally ill for most of your childhood? Most of us will instinctively behave with our children the way our parents behaved with us. This is great if your parents were warm, caring people who knew about the needs of a small child and were able to make sure those needs were met. Unfortunately, many parents have not had a great childhood – and this may show in the way they treat their own children.

Neglectful parents may be deliberately choosing not to look after a child properly. Maybe they didn't want children in the first place, and they are just a nuisance that gets in the way of all the things the parents want to do. Maybe they blame a child, unfairly, for things that are going wrong in their own lives. Or maybe they just can't be bothered, and make themselves the most important people in their lives, putting the child much further down in the pecking order. Perhaps they know perfectly well how to look after children, and are doing just that with some of their children. But there is the one child they don't feel is worth the effort, one child they just don't feel the same way about, and that child becomes the neglected one.

On the other hand, neglectful parents may love their children dearly. They may be doing their best, but they may not really have a clue how to do a proper job as parents. They don't know what the right foods are, or that a baby needs to be held and talked to, or that dangerous things need to be kept high, out of a toddler's reach. They may be struggling to survive on very little money and not know how to budget to make sure there is enough food and clothing to go around. Or they may be working very long hours, always stressed and in a rush, and they may not feel they have enough time to do everything. Their housing might be in very bad repair, with damp everywhere and mould growing on the walls, which makes keeping clothes clean and dry just about impossible. And regular baths and hair-washes are not easy when there's no hot water in the house.

Of course, it is possible to look after your children perfectly well in the most appalling conditions. But it is much more difficult. The more difficult life is, the more important it is that you have the sort of skills and knowledge of young children that will help you to protect them from the worst effects of the environment they are living in. If you haven't got the skills and knowledge, there is more chance of neglect.

Recognising neglect

Most of the neglect cases social workers deal with do not cause death or serious physical harm. But the neglect drags on for weeks or months so that the child is not able to develop the way a child of that age should.

You are more likely to spot neglect in young children than in teenagers, because the older children are, the more power they have to help themselves. Babies and small children have to rely on adults to make sure they are well-fed, warm and clean enough to stay healthy. So if you see a child who is always filthy and smelly, whose clothes don't seem to get changed for ages and whose hair is always tangled and dirty, that might be a child to talk to someone you trust about. A neglected child might also be very hungry all the time. (Lots of children claim to be hungry, but they would not be prepared to eat whatever was offered. The neglected child might try to steal food, or eat other people's leftovers or pick food up from the floor or even out of the bin.)

You might spot neglect in a small child who doesn't get a nappy change anything like as often as needed, and will smell and have very sore skin or rashes. Neglected children might also be very, very tired all the time and feel poorly with illnesses that parents seem to be ignoring.

You might come across a child who is pale, pinch-faced and desperate for food because no-one at home is feeding them. Or a child might be sent out in the freezing cold with no warm clothing. Or you might realize that a neighbour has left small children alone in the home while they go out.

If you are worried about a child – or a friend – that you think might be neglected, talk to someone you trust. See p.65 for more telephone and website contacts that might help.

What do you think?

Although we usually think about neglect as something that goes on for a long time, sometimes a one-off incident is enough to make the offence a criminal one. Read the newspaper story from the Daily Telegraph about the trial of Christiana Ribas. What do you think of what she did? Do you think she intended to harm her baby, thought the baby would be all right, or just didn't care? Was the sentence a fair one?

Mother left baby in car to drink at nightclub

By Nigel Bunyan

A mother left her 18-month-old daughter locked in a car for five hours while she got drunk in a nightclub, a court heard.

Christiana Ribas, 28, staggered out to her car at 2.20 a.m. on a cold February night and tried to drive away.

It was only when club doormen stopped her that the baby, dressed only in shorts and a thin top, was spotted in the back seat of Ribas's Volkswagen Golf.

Ribas, of Salford, Greater Manchester, was jailed for three months after a district judge said her treatment of her baby was one of the most "shameful" episodes of child cruelty he had dealt with.

The court heard how Ribas, a first-year IT student at Manchester Metropolitan University, drove to the city's Elemental nightclub on Feb 20.

She parked outside about 9.30 p.m. and danced and drank for five hours.

Janet Hall, prosecuting, said Ribas became aggressive when the doorman took her car keys. Shortly before the police arrived a doorman noticed the baby, whose presence had been missed because the car had blacked-out windows.

Ribas pleaded guilty to charges of child cruelty, failing to take a breath test, and driving with no insurance.

Physical Abuse

Kicking   punching   hitting

poisoning   shaking   burning

Physical abuse involves doing things like hitting, shaking, punching, kicking, deliberately scalding or burning a child. It can also mean picking up and throwing a child, or giving adult medicines or other substances that might poison a child. There are some parents who deliberately half-drown or half-suffocate their children. Lots of physical abuse cases come out of situations where the child is being punished for being naughty, but the punishment goes way over the top and the child is left injured.

Physical abuse can be something that only happens once – a parent flies into a rage and beats the child up, or hits the child so hard that bones are broken – or it can be something that happens lots of times over a long period. Many parents don't actually mean to hurt their children. They lose control because they are stressed out about other things, or because a crying baby has left them sleepless and exhausted and at breaking point. But some parents coldly and deliberately set out to torture their children. And there are all sorts of people in between, who go over the top now and then in the way that they punish their children, or need some help in how to use discipline safely.

Some parents, usually mothers, pretend that a child is ill. They will even take the child to the doctor seeking treatment for this 'illness'. The doctor may have prescribed harmful medicine or even surgical treatment in hospital before anyone realizes that the parent is lying. This behaviour is called 'factitious illness' or 'Munchausen's syndrome by proxy'. Parents do it to get attention for themselves. In the more extreme type of this behaviour, parents will actually make their children ill or even kill them, by giving them poisonous substances or rubbing things on their skin, for example.

What do you think?

Read about Petrina Stocker (below), who poisoned her son.

MOTHER FACES JAIL FOR KILLING SON BY PUTTING SALT IN FEEDS

By Sue Clough, Courts Correspondent

A mother who killed her nine-year-old son by putting salt in his milk feed drip while he was a patient in Great Ormond Street Hospital is facing jail today.

Petrina Stocker, 42, who as a teenager faked a skin disease by putting acid on her face, arms and legs to gain attention and later feigned other illnesses, showed little emotion yesterday as an Old Bailey jury convicted her of manslaughter.

Before putting 18 teaspoons of salt into the feed of her son, David, she had interfered with samples taken from him in the months leading up to his death in August 2001. The court heard that her behaviour was typical of fabricated and induced illness (FII), which was known as Munchausen's syndrome by proxy. "She wanted to receive attention by presenting her child at hospital," said Det Chief Inspector Geoff Baker afterwards.

David was a fit, healthy boy at the beginning of 2001 but he became ill and doctors at Oldchurch hospital in Romford, Essex, were unable to diagnose his illness. Stocker had been interfering with samples taken from him.

He spent time at Great Ormond Street, where specialists believed he was suffering from a rare disease that attacked his immune system, and Oldchurch again before returning to Great Ormond Street.

By this time he was little more than a skeleton, sometimes crying out in pain. Staff decided Stocker should never be left alone with her son but she would go to the ward kitchen and add salt to milk feeds stored in a fridge.

Soon after David absorbed it through a drip, he went into a coma and died two days later when his heart stopped.

Stocker will be sentenced today.

Petrina Stocker was eventually sentenced to 5 years in prison. The judge, Gerald Gordon, said, "There has to be some force, incomprehensible to me and most people, driving a mother to behave towards their child as you did."
But what was this "force"? Do you think Petrina Stocker is mentally ill, or is she a cold, deliberate abuser?

Physical abuse is mostly about what a parent *does*, while neglect is mostly about what a parent *doesn't do*. But that's not always the case. Say one parent is violent and regularly abuses a child. If the other parent knows, but doesn't do anything to protect the child – doesn't call for help, doesn't try to stop what's happening – that parent might be accused of abuse, too. Sometimes where one parent is violent to a child, he or she is also violent to the other parent as well. The other parent might be frightened and abused and unable to call for help at the time, just like the child. This is known as *domestic violence*, and it is covered in more detail on p.36. But that parent would still be expected to go for help once the immediate danger is over, to stop it happening again and again.

Recognizing Physical Abuse

When you see a bruise or a cut or some other physical injury, perhaps on a friend or on a child you are babysitting, it is an automatic caring response to ask how it happened. Almost always, the answer will show clearly that it was an accident. But how might you tell if an injury has been caused deliberately by someone else?

There are several ways that non-accidental injuries can be spotted. One of the most obvious is that the explanation given does not fit. Your friend says he has fallen off his bike, but how does that explain a black eye and no other injuries? Or a young child you are babysitting says she fell over but the bruises on her arm look more as though someone has grabbed her really hard.

Someone who is being physically abused may try to hid it e.g. by wearing long sleeved, full length clothes even in Summer, or lying about how the injury happened, even though it is not their fault and they have no power to stop it. They might also be very reluctant to tell anyone – even a close friend – because of what might happen if the person abusing them finds out they've told.

If you are worried about someone you know, perhaps a friend or someone you babysit, talk to an adult you trust or turn to p.65 for telephone numbers and websites that may help.

Smacking – Right or Wrong?

The laws about smacking have recently changed in Great Britain. In Scotland (which has its own laws and legal system, different to the rest of G.B.), a new law in October 2003 banned hitting any child around the head, shaking, or punishing a child with a belt, cane or any other implement. If the child is under the age of three, they must not be hit at all. In England and Wales the law also changed, but not in quite the same way. From January 2005 it became a criminal offence to smack a child hard enough to leave an injury, but parents still have the right to smack their children, whatever their age, as long as they don't go too far.

This right for a parent to smack a child is called the right of 'reasonable chastisement'. The story goes that back in Queen Victoria's day the legal definition of 'reasonable' was described in this way:
If an ordinary working man on the bus in Clapham (let's call him Joe Bloggs) would be likely to say that what you did was reasonable, the law will say it's reasonable too. But if Joe Bloggs would say you went too far, then the law will call it unreasonable and you will therefore have broken the law.

This word 'reasonable' crops up regularly in our laws. We talk about 'reasonable force' (you are allowed to use reasonable force against a burglar, or someone who is trying to attack you). Then there's 'reasonable suspicion' that allows a police officer to stop your car or get a search warrant. And 'reasonable doubt' – if a jury feels any of that, you can't be found guilty of a crime you're being tried for. It is not always very clear where the boundaries of 'reasonable' are, and often court cases will be fought to decide whose idea of what's 'reasonable' is the right one.

Back to smacking. Generally, smacking a child once with the palm of your hand on a part of the body that's got padding – the bottom or the legs, say – is more likely to be reasonable than not.

Smacking a child around the head, or punching, or smacking so hard a bruise is left on the skin, or smacking over and over – all these things are likely to be seen as 'unreasonable' and they would be called abuse.

The age of the child is important too. The younger the child, the easier it is for a smack to cause injury, so the more likely it would be for the smack to be called abuse (and if it happens in Scotland and the child is under three, it would be a criminal offence in any case).

In some countries of the world physical discipline is much harsher, and it would be acceptable to punish a naughty child by beating the child with a stick or hitting hard enough to leave a visible injury. But families who live in the United Kingdom, whatever their nationality or cultural background, have to follow the laws in this country.

Organizations such as the NSPCC and many people who work with children say that smacking should be banned completely. It is already against the law for anyone who works with children, including teachers, foster parents and childminders, to smack any child in their care. The NSPCC and others say this law should cover parents, too. They say it is too easy for violence to get out of hand, and that parents who smack are really only teaching their children that the bigger and stronger you are, the easier it is to get your own way.

Smacking has already been banned in several other European countries. One of the first was Sweden. In the whole time since the law changed there, more than twenty years ago, four children have died at the hands of their parents. In the U.K. that figure is startlingly higher: about one child every week.

However, many parents fought against the change in the law, insisting that mild smacking was not harmful to the child and was a good teaching tool. Many remembered being smacked by their parents as children and were adamant that it had not done them any harm. Indeed, they argued, a short, sharp smack was very effective in teaching them right from wrong.

What do you think?

Discuss your own views about smacking with people in your class. Do you think it should be completely banned? When you are a parent, do you think you will be worried about using a smack, or do you think it's a good way to teach the child to behave properly?

Here are two examples of smacking that reached the court a few years ago, before the change to the law described above. In both cases it was claimed that the parent had gone beyond 'reasonable chastisement' and actually assaulted their children. Guess what the outcome was, and then see if you're right.

Case 1

In Hampshire in 1993, a mother smacked her nine-year-old daughter's bare bottom with a slipper. The child had been caught stealing sweets.

Case 2

In Lanarkshire in 1999, a father smacked his 8 year old daughter's bare bottom with his hand when she refused to go into the dentist's surgery to have a tooth removed; she was afraid of the injection.

Result 2
The man was also found guilty of assault. Although he was only given a warning, he was sacked from his job as a teacher because of the case.

Result 1
The mother was convicted of assault, but she appealed and the verdict was overturned. Judge Ian McClean said, "If a parent cannot slipper a child, the world is going potty."

18

Sexual Abuse

"I thought for a long time that what was happening was O.K. because Dad said it was a game that all fathers played with their sons, a secret game that only the men knew about."

Sexual abuse is to do with someone older, bigger, stronger and/or more powerful using that power to control or humiliate someone in his own family or in a family he is involved with. We generally say 'he' when we talk about sexual abusers because they are usually male – but not always. Women can be abusers too, either by themselves or helping a man to abuse. The abuser is almost always someone the child knows well, and trusts, and may love very much.

The definition used by people who work with sexually abused children says, 'Sexual abuse involves forcing or enticing a young child or young person to take part in sexual activities, whether or not the child is aware of what is happening.'
(Remember that legally, you are a child until your eighteenth birthday. Sexual abuse can happen to a child of any age, even babies and teenagers over sixteen).

'Sexual activities' covers just about anything where the adult (or much older child) is doing something with or to the child for no other reason than to give the abuser some kind of sexual satisfaction. It could be showing or taking pornographic pictures, touching the child's private parts or making the child touch the abuser in a sexual way. It might be teaching sex games or making children do sexual things to each other while the abuser watches. Or it might be putting things into a girl's vagina or a girl or boy's anus. Or it might be actual rape, where the abuser has full sex with the child. The child becomes simply something for the abuser to use; the abuser takes away the child's rights over his or her own body and the power to choose what to do with it. This sense of not being a living, valuable person is one of the reasons why sexual abuse can be difficult to recover from.

Sexual abusers are often clever at making the child feel that it is somehow the child's fault that the abuse happened, or that if people found out about the abuse they would blame the child, or think the child was dirty or disgusting. Perhaps they have bribed the child with money or presents in the past, and use this to say the child is just as guilty. Perhaps they will simply point out to the child that no-one is likely to believe such a story. If the child feels somehow even partly to blame, or thinks there is no-one to tell who will believe what's happening, the secret is more likely to be kept and the abuse can continue.

Sexual abuse is not about grabbing children off the street or from the park and attacking them – that is a straightforward, criminal sexual assault case that will be dealt with by the police. Those attackers do not know the child at all, and just grab a complete stranger. Police will investigate and try to find and punish the attacker just as for any other crime. But almost all abuse – 85% at least – comes from a member of the family or someone close to the family. Most often it will be a father or stepfather, the mother's boyfriend or an older brother. It could also be a close family friend, neighbour or relative.

When sexual abuse happens in the family or close to it, it can be particularly important for Social Services and the police to work together. While the police are gathering the evidence to help them work out what has happened and whether someone should be prosecuted in court for the crime, the social worker will be trying to make sure the child can be kept safe at home, or trying to find someone the child can stay with while the family sorts itself out.

Sexual abuse is very difficult to prove in criminal court and many abusers do not go to prison, although they may be prevented from being with the children they have abused by rulings made in the civil courts (the difference between civil and criminal courts is explained on p.58).

Sometimes a child who is sexually abused will grow up to be an abuser too. But this is not usually the case. Victims of sexual abuse may have a hard time making relationships with other people, especially with girlfriends or boyfriends, because they find it hard to trust anyone. Close contact, like kissing and making love, is difficult and might bring back bad memories of the abuse. Then there's the confusion about whether or not they could have, or should have, done something to stop the abuse happening. The abuser has told them so often that it was their fault, they need lots of reassurance that it wasn't.

Recognising sexual abuse

In very young children, sexual abuse might show itself in their play. If you are babysitting a young child who seems to know a lot about sex, or wants to play sexy games, that is something you might want to check out with an adult you trust. In teenagers, sexual abuse sometimes shows itself in depression, eating disorders, self-injury or not being able to sleep. But all these signs could be down to other things that have nothing to do with abuse.

Sexual abuse is the most difficult abuse to talk about. Most of the time, if you are worried about a friend, all you can do is make sure your friend knows you can be counted on to help if ever the time comes, whatever the problem might be. And if a friend does confide in you, listen calmly. Try not to interrupt. Encourage them to get help, and offer to go with them to tell a teacher or some other trusted person. Make sure your friend knows that you are still their friend, whatever happened. Often, people who have been sexually abused think it must somehow be their fault, or that they should have been able to stop it. Your friend needs to know that it is not in any way their fault, and that telling you has been the first step in stopping it – but you need to find someone who is experienced in this kind of situation, who will know how to help you.

If you are worried that someone you know might be being sexually abused, talk to someone you trust. Look at p.65 for telephone numbers and websites that may help, too.

Paedophiles
(pronounced pee-doh-files)

Some abusers abuse a small number of children, maybe just within their own family. Others abuse literally hundreds of children over many years, finding their victims in their neighbourhood, at work, on the Internet or on holidays, for example. These abusers of many children are called paedophiles, and you have probably heard something about them from the television or newspapers. They appear to be really nice people who can be totally trusted. And they're very good at making friends with children. (This is called 'grooming'). They move into the child's circle of people. Once they are known and trusted, the abuse starts. Paedophiles are dangerous people for children to be around, particularly if they join up with other paedophiles and start swapping pornography and names and addresses of children, or get together to help each other find and abuse children. They are very difficult to catch, especially if children are too frightened to tell anyone what is happening. But police can be clever too, and have more and more sophisticated ways of dealing with paedophiles.

An example of police tactics was Operation Ore. This started in the USA in 2002, when FBI agents tracked 250,000 people who used their credit cards to view a child abuse site on a Texas web portal. These users came from all over the world, so the FBI passed on the details to police forces world-wide. More than 7,000 people were traced to the U.K. By 2005, police had arrested more than 3,500 and charged about 2,000. This kind of co-operation, and the growth of highly trained police who are very experienced in computer technology, would not have been possible a few years ago, but it is now making it easier to catch paedophiles who try to use Internet websites. Detectives regularly catch a crop of paedophiles simply by setting up a fake 'porno' site and tracing people who log on.

Another way that paedophiles use the Internet is by making friends with children in chat rooms. The thing about people you meet in a chat room is that you can't see each other; you can pretend to be whoever you want to be. Paedophiles who use the Internet are very good at pretending to be children or teenagers. A 45 year old man, say, can make himself sound like a twelve year old girl or a sixteen year old boy, or a younger child if necessary. So one side of the conversation is honest and one side is a pack of lies. The paedophile finds out what interests the victim, what they like or dislike and so on, and he will pretend that he feels just the same. So it seems the two people are of the same age and have a lot in common. Only after really getting to know the person he has made contact with does the paedophile suggest meeting up. Usually there will be some reason, cleverly suggested, why the meeting should be in secret so parents don't get to find out. The paedophile will then make his own plans about what to do when the horrified child or teenager turns up at the meeting point and realises – too late – that it was a terrible trick.
(Remember that we use 'he' because it will most often be a man, but there are women involved, too).

What do you think?

How do you stay safe when you're on the Internet, particularly in a chat room?

Write down your top tips for staying safe when you're entering chat rooms, and compare them with the National Children's Home advice on p.66 at the back of the book.

Or

Design a really eye-catching screen saver that includes a catchy slogan about staying safe.

Emotional Abuse

Ever find yourself snapping and snarling at someone when they've done nothing to deserve it? They just happened to be in the wrong place at the wrong time. You were angry or frustrated about something and you needed to take it out on somebody. Hopefully, when you came to your senses and realized that you had gone over the top, you apologized and were forgiven.

You have probably also been on the receiving end of that kind of behaviour, from family or friends. It feels awful – humiliation, anger and hurt can all explode together at the unfairness of it. But it's totally out of character for that person, and you know you have days like that too. So you forgive and, hopefully, forget.

Human beings are not perfect. We're all a bundle of hopes, fears, joys and distresses and, particularly when we're stressed, we're a bit combustible. The occasional blow-up is not pleasant, but as we're growing up we gradually learn that it's a part of life, and that we can get over it.

Some children, though, live with constant explosions; there aren't really any good times. They are told, constantly, that they are no good at anything, that they're a waste of space, ugly, stupid and so on. Or they are completely ignored, because the parent can't be bothered and doesn't care how they feel or what they want. There's no comfort, no encouragement. A small child who falls over and is injured is told to get up and stop making such a fuss. A teenager who has failed an exam is told that nobody ever expected they would pass anyway. A child who wants to try something new is told not to bother; they're bound to be useless at it.

Sometimes emotional abuse is seen in the way a parent will have hopeless expectations of what a child can do. For example, a two year old is told they mustn't get out of bed before 7 o'clock in the morning. They are given a clock to put by their bed. But no two-year-old can tell the time; chances are they will get out of bed at 5 o'clock, thinking the clock says 7, and be punished for being naughty. But they haven't been naughty, they've just been a two year old. So they will become very confused. If things like this keep happening, they will become frightened to do anything new, because it might be 'naughty' and they might be punished for it.

Another form of emotional abuse is when a parent uses a child as a weapon or a tool for something the adult wants. Perhaps the parents have split up, and the child is being used to ferry messages between them and is constantly being told, by each parent, how rotten the other parent is. If they want to see the parent they are not living with, they are made to feel that this is a rejection of the parent they live with. So they learn to keep quiet about their own needs – it causes too much hassle at home.

It's difficult to develop into a healthy, happy, warm and loving person if nobody has shown you what warm and loving means. That's why emotional abuse is so damaging, and that's why it is a part of the child protection procedures. But it's important to remember that emotional abuse is not about stressed-out parents being unfair now and then and sparking awful rows with their children. The law describes emotional abuse as: *persistent emotional ill-treatment of a child such as to cause severe and persistent adverse effects on the child's emotional development.'* In other words, the abuse happens so often, and over such a long time, that the child can't develop in the way a child should: the abuse has stunted their growth, emotionally. They might be so frightened of making someone angry that their behaviour is ruled by the need to keep that person calm. Or they might be completely ignored by the adults at home, which means they don't know how to be in conversations, play games and so on.

There are a lot of similarities between emotional abuse and neglect. They both happen over a long period of time and they cross over quite often. After all, if you are emotionally abusing a child you are neglecting the emotional needs the child has. And if you neglect a child's physical needs the child may get the message of being unloved and unwanted. Another thing that they have in common is that, quite often, the parents don't actually know they are being abusive; they don't mean it. They've just got so caught up in their own problems – or they have so little knowledge about what's involved in bringing up a child – that they've caused damage without even trying.

Recognizing Emotional Abuse

Some children's answer to emotional abuse is to cut off from the world, which has become a hurtful place. They may rock to and fro obsessively, (especially younger children) or not join in anything the other children are up to. They might become depressed, and not have any energy to do anything. Or they might just develop a 'don't care' attitude, doing whatever they want and not caring about other people's reactions. Some, especially teenagers, react to emotional abuse – and to other kinds of abuse too – by trying to hurt themselves. This is called self-harm, and is explored in a bit more detail on p.34.

What emotionally abused people tend to have in common is that they have almost no self esteem, just the certainty that they will never be any good at anything and that they are not likeable or lovable people. This lack of self esteem can come from other causes, as well as from abuse, but it is a very difficult thing to deal with if you are the family or friend of such a person. You keep trying to show them the great person you know they really are, but they simply won't believe it.

If you are worried that someone you know may be suffering emotional abuse, talk to an adult you trust or turn to p.53 for advice on what to do to get help.

What do you think?

What makes you blow? How much stress can you take? Think of some times when you have been really unfair to someone while you're stressed out.

Is there a pattern e.g. do you always react in the same sort of way?

Who do you take it out on when things are bad, and how do you make up afterwards?

Can you recognise the signals that stress is getting out of control?

What can you do to stop yourself getting into a real state? Swap ideas with a few friends or classmates for staying cool under pressure.

Why Don't People Tell About Abuse?

It's the obvious question, isn't it? Children, teenagers and adults too seem to choose a lifetime of physical and mental pain, shame and degradation rather than tell someone and get help. It is easy to become frustrated and angry with a friend, however much we feel for them, who refuses to take action that would end the abuse. But is it that simple? Do they really have a choice?

One of the hardest things to come to terms with, when we think about child abuse, is the damage it does inside the person. Abuse can take away your whole sense of who you are and how much power you have. You can become convinced that you are not worth helping, that no-one will listen or believe you, that no-one will be able to help.

Here are some of the reasons people commonly give for not telling about their abuse straight away.

- ○ Some children, particularly young ones, don't know that they are being abused. They think this happens in every family.
- ○ Shame is a common feeling among abused people. Although the abuse is not their fault in any way, they feel they must have done something to provoke it; the abuser will tell them that, too.
- ○ Love is a very strange thing: it is possible to love someone even though they are doing awful things to you, particularly if sometimes they are kind and loving. So children might keep quiet to protect the abuser.
- ○ If abuse has gone on for a long time, perhaps from before the child could recognise it as abuse, it's even harder to tell. People will ask the obvious question, 'Why didn't you tell before?' The child knows this question will be asked, and just doesn't know the answer.

- ○ Bribes, threats and tricks are quite common in child abuse, particularly in sexual abuse. If the child accepted a bribe, or was tricked into something abusive, they might feel guilty and ashamed. If there is a threat e.g. to kill someone in the family, the fear of what might happen is stronger than the need to tell.
- ○ Sometimes, children think they have told. For example, they might have said they didn't like so-and-so and nobody took any notice. Children tell in strange ways, sometimes. If this isn't recognised by adults at the time, the child can end up thinking the adults know all about it.
- ○ We can all tell when someone we are talking to is uncomfortable with what we're saying, and wishes we would stop. If a child starts to tell and gets that kind of signal, particularly with sexual abuse, they might stop to protect the adult.

So what helps people to tell, in the end? Again, here are some of the most common reasons given:

- ○ The abuse just becomes too unbearable – the fear of it becomes more powerful than the abuse itself. This fear might be particularly strong if the child feels that 'next time' they might be very badly hurt, or in sexual abuse there might be a risk of pregnancy.
- ○ The abused child finds out that brothers or sisters are also being abused, and tells to protect them.
- ○ Quite simply, the child finds someone who is easy to tell, someone they think will have more power than the abuser. Often, it will be someone that the child senses has a hunch something is wrong, which makes it easier to talk.
- ○ The child is so badly injured, or ill, that a doctor or hospital recognises something is wrong. (Sometimes sexual abuse is picked up when a child becomes pregnant, for example).

Crime and Punishment

Below are three snapshots of children who have done something they shouldn't have. Imagine you are the parent, and you have to decide what to do. Discuss with others in your class or at home, and see how much agreement or disagreement there is.

Look at the list of actions, and decide which would be suitable in each case. Are there any things mentioned that you would never want to do? Why not?

You can use the possible actions as many times as you like, but you don't have to use any of them. You can also add your own ideas – but smacking is not allowed, nor is any kind of physical punishment.

Before you decide on your actions, be clear about your reasons for choosing it. If your answer is going to start with, 'It depends . . . ' be clear what it depends upon.

Try to choose an action that will:
- ○ Show the child that what they have done is not acceptable.
- ○ Matches the seriousness of what was done.
- ○ Takes into account the age and understanding of the child.

The 'crimes'

Karim, aged 2, has picked the heads off all the flowers in the garden and collected them in his toy wheelbarrow to make a flower pie for tea.

Sally, aged 3 has snatched her 1 year old sister's biscuit and pushed her over. Twice.

Jed, aged 4, knows he is not allowed out of the garden. But when you went in to answer the 'phone, he slipped out of the gate and is on his way to the local shop.

Tara, aged 7, has taken her 15 year old sister's make-up and perfume and is playing dressing up with it: most of the perfume is gone and the make-up is ruined.

Mary and Martin, aged 10 and 11, had a big fight in the living room. It ended when they crashed into a shelf and smashed a glass vase full of flowers and a china bowl.

Jon, aged 12, has come home an hour later than he was told to for the third time in a week.

Perry, 13, stole £5 from his mum's purse to buy cider. He and his friend are brought home by a neighbour who found them, drunk, in the park.

Jade, 15, said she was staying at a friend's house. The friend told her parents she was staying at Jade's house. But a chance conversation with Jade's mum shows this to be a lie. In fact, they went to a night club and then went back to an older friend's house when the club finished at 4 a.m.

The 'punishments'

Explain why this was a bad thing to do, and ask the child not to do it again.

Explain that it was a bad thing to do, and warn that it must never happen again.

Shout at the child and make sure they know how angry and upset you are.

Tell the child what they have done has made you really angry.

Say what will happen if they do it again.

Ignore the child completely (for how long?).

Send the child to their room (for how long?).

Take away a favourite toy or possession (for how long?).

Stop the child doing something they like e.g. watching television or playing on the computer (for how long?).

Lock the child up in a room or cupboard until you are sure they are sorry.

Make the child pay for any damage caused.

Make the child pay a fine, or lose pocket money (how much?).

Make the child do household chores as a way of saying sorry.

Ground the child (for how long?).

Self-harm

20% of deaths in young people are suicides.

About 142,000 hospital admissions in England and Wales every year are the result of self-harm. About 19,000 of them are children and teenagers.

Sometimes, especially in older children and teenagers, there is a need to do something deliberately to cause an injury: cutting, burning, bruising and so on. This is discussed here because it is sometimes a response to abuse. But not everybody who self-harms (and research suggests there are quite a lot of people) does it because they have been emotionally abused. Self-harm comes from deep unhappiness. That might have been caused by some kind of trauma such as rape, or the death of someone close, or witnessing a terrible event, but there can be many reasons why people start.

If you have a friend who is deliberately self-harming, it can seem a stupid and dangerous thing to do. But for the self-harmer, it provides a strange sort of comfort. Here is what three people who regularly cut or burn themselves have to say about it:

Katy, 14:
"I like knowing that it's <u>me</u> causing the pain for once, not someone else. I'm in control."

Daniel, 16:
You get this build-up of panic and anxiety . . . I feel like I'm going to explode inside. Then I cut myself, and somehow it lets it all out. I feel calmer. Also, I think a pain that you can see, and you know why it's there, is less scary than a pain inside that you don't understand."

Nilufar, 12:
I don't really know why I do it. There's this nagging feeling that I'm such a no-hoper, and so bad, that I deserve to be punished. And it's a way of showing people something's wrong, even when I pretend I'm O.K."

Self-harm is a dangerous habit to form, whatever triggers it. Whether it's to do with abuse or some other cause, self-harm is a sign that someone needs help.

If you, or a friend, are self-harming, try to talk to an adult you trust about it, perhaps a teacher or school nurse. Or you could contact one of the organisations on the Numbers and Webs page (p.65) You will find someone there who will listen and understand, without judging, and who will try to help you without forcing you to do anything you don't want to do. It will also be O.K. to stay anonymous, if you're not ready to tell your family what's happening.

Domestic Violence

YOU BROKE HER JAW BECAUSE SUPPER WASN'T READY ...

TRY TELLING THAT TO THE JUDGE
domestic violence is a crime

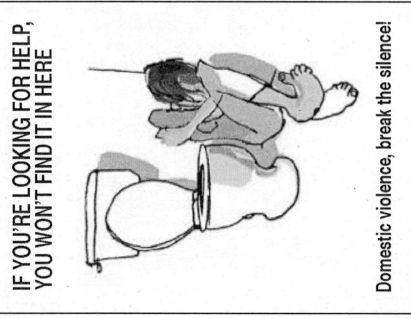

IF YOU'RE LOOKING FOR HELP, YOU WON'T FIND IT IN HERE

Domestic violence, break the silence!

> *One incident of domestic violence is reported to the police every minute.*
>
> *On average, one woman dies every three days as a result of domestic violence.*
>
> *Almost always (about 90% of the time) children are present in the same home when domestic violence happens.*
>
> *About half the time, when parents are violent to each other children are hurt, too.*
>
> *Approximately 2000 children contact Childline every year about domestic violence going on at home.*

There is not a crime that is called 'domestic violence', but these words describe a range of crimes that can happen in a family between adults (as opposed to child abuse crimes). The Government says domestic violence is:

Any incident of threatening behaviour, violence or abuse (physical, sexual, financial or emotional) between adults who are or have been intimate members or family members, regardless of gender or sexuality.

So the definition of 'family' when we talk about domestic violence includes mum, dad, brother, sister, grandparents, in-laws, stepfamily, and partners who are not married, whether it's a man and a woman, or a gay/lesbian relationship. The people involved have to be 18 or over. Abuse happening to children (under 18) is dealt with by different laws and procedures.

Most domestic violence is committed by a man against a woman, and that's the way this book will talk about it. But it's important to know that there are cases where a woman terrorises or physically hurts a male partner.

Domestic violence happens in all kinds of families and across all age ranges, cultural and ethnic groups, income groups etc. No matter where you live, whether you're rich or poor, white, black or Asian, religious or not, look at the statistics above and you'll realize that you are never very far from domestic violence. On any one day, there are literally millions of people trying to live with it, or escape it. So, there's a real chance that you, or a friend or a neighbour, may one day need the information in this section.

Kinds of violence

We often think about violence as a physical thing – punching, kicking, stabbing and so on. But as the Government's definition shows, there are many ways to be violent and not all of them involve physical contact. Domestic violence is mostly about control – the man seeks to control the woman and have complete power over her. So he does whatever he can to get and keep that control. But many of these abusers also have days when they are kind, caring, funny and great to be with. They feel really bad about what they have done and beg for forgiveness; they promise that it will never, ever, happen again. So the family thinks everything will be O.K. – this time, they say, he really means it. They start to trust the abuser – until the next time (and there will always be a next time).

Physical violence

This involves much the same kind of behaviour as that we looked at in child abuse; hitting, pushing, kicking and so on. Usually the violence is so bad that it leaves the victim with visible injuries (although they might be on parts of the body that can be hidden under clothing). Injuries might require medical assistance and, in extreme forms, domestic violence ends up in murder. Physical violence is frequently linked to being drunk.

Sexual violence

Again, there are a lot of similarities with child abuse. Sexual violence means forcing someone to take part in any sexual behaviour (not just full sex) that makes them feel uncomfortable; sex without consent is rape, even if the two people are married.

Emotional violence

This has a lot to do with control; making sure the woman has no belief in herself or in the willingness of anyone else to help her. If you constantly tell someone she is stupid, worthless, ugly, stinking and completely unattractive, she will eventually believe it (particularly if she loves you and believes you love her). She will believe you are the only person who will put up with her, and become so frightened of losing you, or so frightened of being hurt again, that she will do anything to stop you getting angry. Friends and relatives are not allowed to visit and the woman is not allowed out, so there is little chance of anyone outside the home being able to persuade her to leave. Many women in this situation are, in fact, prisoners, and need to plot their escape as carefully as if they were escaping from jail.

Financial control

Many domestic violence abusers control their wives/partners completely, even down to making sure she never has any money of her own. She is not allowed to have a job – or is checked up on several times a day and never dares be late home. Money earned is immediately handed over and the man is in control of every penny spent.

How domestic violence affects children

If you live in a home where there is violence between your parents, you are at a high risk of physical abuse yourself. You might try and step in to stop a parent being hurt; you might get in the way accidentally or the parent might be so enraged that they deliberately turn on you. There are also occasions when the children will be hurt or threatened in front of the mother in order to get at her.

Even if you are not physically hurt, the emotional torment of watching your mother being beaten up, or hearing it happen from another room, can stay with you for the rest of your life. Here are some of the feelings children and teenagers told Childline about, when they called to talk about domestic violence.

I think we blamed ourselves for the violence because he used to hit her (mum) if he didn't have enough money for drink, but we were eating the money coz it was for food.

Sandra, now an adult

Dad hits me and Mum most days. He's always hit us. He doesn't work and drinks all day. I want it to stop. I'm so unhappy. Dad says he will kill us if we leave.

Gerry, aged 12

Why doesn't Mum leave her boyfriend? She's not happy. When I asked her, she said I'm too young to understand.

Mark, 14

Going to a Refuge (Safe House)

A refuge, sometimes known as a safe house, is a place women and children can go to escape from violence at home. It is a secure place, where no unwanted visitor can get in. The refuge has staff who can help sort out the problems that come with leaving home because of violence: counselling, finding somewhere else to live, registering with a doctor and a school, getting financial help and so on. Some refuges are small blocks of flats, others are big houses where the family has its own bedrooms but shares the kitchen, living room etc. with other families in the house. The refuge can supply food, nappies, soap and so on for families who have had to leave so suddenly they were not able to pack anything. The local police will help a family get to a refuge, if it becomes necessary. Families stay anything from a few days to a few months – however long it takes to get started again and to feel safe.

What you can do

If you are worried about domestic violence, check out the website noted on p.65 (Numbers and webs page). It gives good advice and suggestions for getting out of violent situations. It also tells you what to do with your computer to make sure that no-one can tell you've been on the website.

In an emergency, a child dealing with domestic violence at home needs to know that if you have started to call 999 when the violent person comes into the room and you don't want to be caught phoning for help, you should not hang up. The police will always call back to check everything is O.K., so the person will know what you've done. The police advice if you are ever in a situation like this is to leave the phone off the hook, so they can hear what's happening. They can trace the call and come to help you.

If you, or a friend, live with domestic violence, make sure your mobile phone is kept in credit. Agree a password that can be used with a trusted friend – if they hear this password, or see it in a text, they will send help, without the violent person knowing the call for help has been made.

Parents and Alcohol or Drug Dependency

"I have to tell her when to go to bed, I have to undress her. She is covered in cuts and bruises and never knows where she gets them – she falls down the stairs. I hate coming home from school – I never know what I'm going to find. I never get used to it."

Marie, aged 14

According to the Health Development Agency, 40% of all admissions to Casualty departments in hospitals are related to alcohol. There are about 150,000 hospital admissions each year for alcohol-related sickness, and about 1/3 of domestic violence and child abuse cases involve abusers who are drunk. About one million children in the U.K. are affected by alcohol mis-use in the family.

When it comes to drugs, there has been a steady increase over the last ten years of people using illegal drugs. There are currently about 1.8 million addicts in the U.K. and 4 million users of illegal drugs in the UK today. (This figure is based on people answering survey questions honestly, and the real figure is probably much higher).

With statistics like that, you would think we would know a lot about alcohol and drug dependency. Lots of the people in those statistics have to be parents. But still, children think it is something only happening in their families, something they must keep quiet about. There is a lot of shame about having an 'addict' in the family, even though it is not in any way the fault of the children.

Living with a parent who is dependent on alcohol or drugs is very tough. When they've been using, the parents might be physically violent and mentally nasty. The next day, that same person can be all smiles and hugs. Many parents who drink heavily manage to hold down jobs and look after their children most of the time. But when things go wrong, and you need a parent to be in charge, it's often the child who has to sort everything out. The child becomes the parent and the parent becomes the child. Some children also have to take care of younger brothers and sisters because they are actually in danger if they are left with a parent who is drunk or stoned. They might be very angry about it, but they're worried about what will happen to the parent if they tell someone what's going on.

Sometimes, the child feels guilty about the parent's dependency, as if they are somehow to blame for it. There are days shut away from school, friends and the outside world because a parent has become violent and left bruises that you don't want anyone to see. Or you live with constant fear about what's going to happen, especially when you're not there. It can be embarrassing to bring friends home, because a drunk or stoned parent might behave really strangely. It's also hard to talk to anyone about what's going on in the family. So it's easy to become depressed, hopeless and angry. There doesn't seem to be any point to life. Some children react by becoming very angry; they want to kill the parent. But there's no way they can express the anger, and they know they won't really harm the parent, because at the same time as being angry they are also desperately worried about what will happen to that parent. So the anger turns back inside and eats away at the child instead.

Sadly, the parent with alcohol or drug dependency is usually the last person to see that there's a problem. Until they do see, it is almost impossible to stop them drinking. Many children who live with this situation will confide in a friend rather admit to an adult that there's something wrong at home. So anyone could become involved. If you, or a friend, find yourself in this situation, what do you need to know, and what can you do?

On the following page are some of the questions that are most frequently asked by children and teenagers contacting Childline or various Internet sites dealing with the problem.

Will I become an addict too?

Is it my fault?

Can I make them stop?

What do you think?

If you were asked these questions by someone whose parents were heavy drinkers or drug users, how would you answer? Use what you already know, and guess what you don't know. Then look at the answers on p.45.

Answers to frequently asked questions (p.44)

Will I become an addict too?

Addiction does tend to run in families. It seems to be partly genetic but it's mostly to do with the environment around you while you're growing up. If you are surrounded by people who drink heavily or use illegal drugs, it is natural to see this kind of behaviour as normal and to start behaving that way yourself.

BUT – and it is a big but – drug or alcohol dependent parents do not necessarily turn their children into users, too. It only means you need to take particularly good care of yourself. Eat as healthily as you can, get involved with sports and lots of other activities that happen at school or outside the home where people are not using drugs or alcohol to make things happen for them. And talk – to friends, to family, trusted adults at school, to drop in centres – to anyone you think might be able to support you. Parents might want you to keep it a secret, but when their behaviour affects your life, it becomes your right to choose whether or not to talk about it, not theirs.

Is it my fault?

Alcohol or drug dependency is a disease. It is not caused by having children around, any more than cancer or arthritis is. But part of the alcohol/drug dependency disease is its effect on the mind and the ability to think straight. Sometimes a parent will try to blame anyone and anything for the state they're in – including their children. That's the disease talking, though. Children do not control adults' behaviour – adults do.

Can I make them stop?

Sadly, no. The parents have to recognise that they're in trouble, and accept that they need help to put things right. If they don't realise their behaviour is out of control, and don't want to change, it's almost impossible for them to stop. The disease blinds them to anything except their own needs. However much they love their children, the addiction has the main power; even

45

if they try to stop, the addiction will overcome them unless they are very, very determined not to let it win.

What you, and other members of the family can do is refuse to make the dependency your problem. Don't hide bottles, don't help them to be users in any way, don't beat yourself up trying to be perfect and don't promise not to tell anyone – that's your decision, no-one else's.

Finding out more

If you have access to the Internet, do a search on "alcoholic parents" or "drug-using parents" for an insight into the world of children living with alcohol or drug dependency in the family.

Discuss what you would want to say to parents who drink heavily but who have not yet become totally dependent. If you only had the chance to make three statements, what would be the most effective in making them think about their drinking? Write them down in the form of a chart, with whatever illustration you think is effective in getting the message across.

Make two or three posters, each one containing a short but powerful message about parents and drug use (see the domestic violence posters on p.36 as an example).

Parents with Mental Illness

About a quarter of us will experience some kind of depression during our lives. For 1 in 10 of us, mental illness will be serious enough to make normal life very difficult.

Of all the illnesses you could have, mental illness is among the most dreaded because it is still a taboo in our society. People don't want to talk about it, don't want to admit they have it and don't want to be around others who have it. It is an illness that remains, for many people, a very secret and very shameful thing. And yet anyone can experience mental illness for a time, however strong, healthy and happy they have been before (or will be afterwards).

If you have a cold, you usually treat it yourself. If it turns into bronchitis, you will probably see a doctor and receive some treatment. If you develop serious pneumonia, you might need hospital treatment. Mental illness works the same way. Some people get mild depression from time to time and have their own ways of dealing with it. Others get it so badly that they need to see a doctor and perhaps get some counselling or some anti-depressant tablets to help them through. But for some people the illness becomes so serious that they need hospital treatment.

When parents have mental health problems, there is bound to be an effect on the children too. Parents might be unable to look after their children properly because they can't think straight, or keep up with what's going on around them, or even find the energy to get out of bed. In fact, family roles can sometimes get reversed; children end up looking after parents, and maybe younger brothers or sisters.

If you are in a single parent family, or both parents have mental illness, there is likely to be poverty, too, as the family struggle to get by on benefits. And life can be very unpredictable. Children need routines, security, and a trustworthy adult to turn to when they have problems. If that adult is trustworthy one day and completely cut off from you the next, life becomes full of the unknown, and quite scary.

The fact that mental illness is not something people like to talk about leads to many other problems for children living with a parent who has mental health problems. The sense of shame – even though it's no-one's fault, and certainly not the child's – makes it difficult to make and keep friends. After all, at some point friends want to find out about your family, visit your house, call you on the telephone...that means a risk of them finding out what life is like at home for you, so you try to avoid making proper friends. Instead, you become very lonely, resentful when you see how other families live, perhaps angry with the ill parent. It isn't logical, but it happens.

What you can do

If you, or a friend, are living with someone who is mentally ill, try not to judge that person by the illness. You wouldn't reject someone just because they had a broken leg, would you? Mental illness is no worse than physical illness, it just sometimes shows itself in an unnerving way – like a huge scary rash, but on the mind rather on the skin.

The best thing you can do is find out about the illness. It's very easy to be misinformed, so make sure your source is a good one. Talk to a doctor or a support group for the illness involved. There almost always is one, full of people who have the same illness and who can answer all your questions and give help and support to the sick person, too. You can also go to the local library and see if there are any helpful books there, or do an Internet search by typing in the name of the illness – or even just the words 'mental illness' or 'mental health'.

Knowledge and Practice

There is a huge variety of illnesses that come under the umbrella heading of 'mental illness'. In pairs or small groups, take one each and find out enough about it to report back to the class with a short presentation (about two minutes). The list below will give you some to choose from, or you may already know about another form of mental illness that you would like to explore.

Depression
Schizophrenia
Bi-polar disorder
Obsessive-compulsive disorder
Agoraphobia
Claustrophobia
Dementia
Alzheimer's disease
Paranoia
Post-traumatic stress disorder

Try to find out as much as you can, and choose whatever feels right for the presentation. For example, you could include:

- The common and scientific names for the illness, if they are different.
- How the illness shows itself (symptoms).
- How many people in the U.K. suffer from it, and whether there are any particular groups more affected than others e.g. more women than men, more older people than younger people, etc.
- The ways the illness is usually treated e.g. drugs or therapy.

After the presentations, discuss the attitudes you and people you know have towards those with mental health problems:

- Are mentally ill people dangerous to themselves or others?
- Should mentally ill people be allowed to have charge of young children?

○ What could be done to make society more accepting of people with mental health problems?

If you are worried about the mental health of someone you know, talk to someone you trust or look at p66 for sources of help.

Racism in the Family

"My stepfather is always hitting me and calling me horrible names because my dad was from Nigeria."

Miriam, 11 years old

Neelam, 16, had a white boyfriend. Her parents found out and beat her severely. She hardly went out at all and a marriage was being planned. She said that her parents had threatened to kill her if she did not agree.

Racism is a nasty thing whether you encounter it out on the streets, from strangers, or from friends and the community. But if your own family are turning against you because of their racist beliefs, it's even harder to deal with. The family home becomes a battleground, and there's nowhere to retreat to.

For some parents, it is taken for granted that children of the family will be forever bound by the same religion or culture as their parents. To step outside these boundaries, and particularly to have boyfriends or girlfriends from other cultures or religions, is seen as a betrayal. Taken to the extreme, it becomes something that must be stopped at all costs. Parents have been known to imprison their children in the home, beat them up or even, rarely, murder them if they won't conform.

Some children are rejected at birth if they are of mixed race. Grandparents, other family members and friends – from either or both sides of the family - may decide to have nothing to do with the baby. And sometimes the child of a mixed race relationship suffers racism when the parents split up and one parent forms a new relationship with a partner of the same race. This leaves the child visibly different from the rest of the family, particularly if the new couple have children too. The child no longer 'fits'.

In most families this is simply not a problem, except for a bit of embarrassment when you are meeting new people and having to explain that yes, this is your family even though you are different colours. But for a minority of parents it leads to rejection of the 'different' child, even though the child is not really different at all and has done absolutely nothing to make this situation happen.

I am black and my mum is white . . . She has a new boyfriend who is completely racist . . . He says things like, "You need a bath".

What can you do?

Racism is not something any of us should tolerate, and if it is happening within a family it is emotional abuse and has to stop. We can all challenge racism whenever we see it happening, and never let a difference in race, culture or religion get in the way of making friends. If you have a good, supportive network of friends and trusted adults to rely on outside your family, it can help you get through things like racism from your own family. So if you have a friend who is suffering from racism, in or outside the family, the best thing you can do is simply be a friend: listen, sympathise, make sure they don't feel they are in any way to blame for racist people's opinions of them. Find help from a trusted adult. See p.65 for people you can talk to about the problems.

Confidentiality: Who Can I Talk To?

If you needed to talk to someone about abuse that you, or a friend, had experienced or which was still going on, who could you talk to, and how far would your conversation go? Choosing the right person to confide in can be very difficult, but it's usually the first step to really dealing with the problem and getting on with your life. A good friend is the most natural choice for many people, but it's difficult to know whether your friend will be able to keep such a huge secret, and in any case will they know what to do to help?

Everyone who has a job that involves working with children and young people has a duty to act if they think there's a risk of harm. These people should have been trained in what child abuse is and what to do about it. It's a bit of a two-edged sword for the child who wants to tell. On the one hand, a teacher or youth worker or school nurse will know exactly who to contact to help you, and will be able to talk to you openly and with knowledge about your kind of situation. They are unlikely to be shocked, and they will take the time to talk to you. On the other hand, they are not allowed to keep what they say to themselves, if they feel you or someone else might be at risk of being harmed.

If what you need is absolute confidentiality, with no risk of anyone finding out who you are or passing on what you tell them, the telephone help-line is the first step. Nobody can see you, and you can give a false name or no name at all. Childline, for example, is well used to people who don't want to say who they are, but who need someone to talk to who will give advice without judging or trying to take over. It's an easy number to remember, too – 0800 1111 - a good one to memorise in case you ever need it, for you or for someone else. Childline is there 24 hours a day, seven days   a week, all year round. But sometimes it's difficult to get through, because there are so many calls. You might need to keep trying.

Another anonymous help line is The Samaritans. They are not just there for suicidal people. They will provide a listening ear for whatever is bringing you down. They can help you sort out how you feel about what's happening and what you want to do. See p.65 for this telephone number and for other sources of help.

Ways to tell

Find a family member, teacher, nurse, neighbour or good friend that you trust and say, 'Can I tell you something that will be really difficult for me to talk about?' and come straight out with it, or at least enough of it to let them know that you need their help. You don't have to tell everything at once, or go into all the gory details.

Write a letter to someone you trust who you think will help you. Sometimes, writing things down is easier than talking.

Use the 'anonymous' box that some schools have to help you with sensitive questions. This is usually in Health or Personal and Social Education lessons, or form time. If you are not sure what is happening is abuse, or if you want to know what to do about it, write it down as a question and see what answer your teacher and/or classmates give, without having to say it's your problem.

Telephone a helpline or contact a website – see all the ones listed on p66. It's up to you whether you stay anonymous, use a false name or give your real one.

Quiz: What Do You Know?

If you have worked your way through the book so far, you should have a good idea of what abuse is. We have looked at the idea of significant harm, and how that can be shown in neglect, physical abuse, sexual abuse and emotional abuse. We have also looked at some of the things that happen in families that might worry people, but they are not serious enough to meet the definition of significant harm.

So have a look at the following situations, and say whether or not you think they are likely to lead to significant harm unless something in the family changes. Your choice of answers is: YES/NO/IT DEPENDS
If your answer is IT DEPENDS, say what it depends upon.

1. Dad forgets to make his 5 year old daughter's packed lunch and she is hungry at school that day.
2. Mum is depressed and stays in bed all day, so 8 year old boy has to look after himself and his 6-month-old baby brother.
3. Dad kisses his children good night as he tucks them into bed.
4. Babysitter tickles children's private parts when she tucks them into bed.
5. Grandmother hits grandchild with a belt when the child is being very naughty.
6. Grandfather smacks child's legs with his open hand when the child is being very naughty.
7. Mum and Dad have blazing row with each other and are then very snappy with their children for the rest of the day.
8. Divorced parents try to get their children to take sides in their rows, and frequently tell them how useless the other parent is.
9. Mum makes child do his homework before he goes out with his friends.
10. Mum clips a child round the ear because he has had a bad school report.

Answers to 'What do You Know?'

1. No - it's one bad day, and hopefully won't happen again. If it went on and on, or the child wasn't being fed at home at all, it would be neglect.

2. Yes – the boy is too young to take care of himself properly, let alone a baby.

3. No – that's what mums and dads should do. We all need cuddles and kisses, especially when we're young – as long as they're safe kisses and cuddles that make us feel secure and loved.

4. Yes – this is sexual abuse, because the babysitter is temporarily taking the parents' place and is someone the child knows and trusts. She is supposed to protect the child.

5. Yes – however naughty the child has been, this is not a suitable punishment. It is physical abuse.

6. No – although there are better ways to show a child right from wrong than by smacking, this would be seen as a family's right to discipline their child, as long as they don't leave any visible injury.

7. No – unfortunately, rows do happen and, although it's not fair, sometimes angry parents can't stop being angry with everyone around them, including children.

8. Yes, this is emotional abuse. Children should not be used in battles between their parents, and trying to involve children in this way can seriously affect them.

9. No – unless Mum takes it to extremes and locks him in his room for hours. Then it could be emotional, or even physical abuse.

10. Probably. (Give yourself a point for Yes or for It depends...). In Scotland, where you are not allowed to hit a child on the head whatever their age, this would be abuse. In the rest of the U.K. it would depend upon things like whether or not the child had an injury, whether it was a one-off or part of a pattern of violence in the family, and so on. But it would certainly be regarded by most child protection workers as an unacceptable way to punish a child.

How many did you score?

Seven or more shows you've got a handle on what abuse is, so well done.

Child Protection Enquiries:
How They Work

Everybody who works with children has a duty to take action when they think those children are being abused or might be at risk of abuse. It's part of their job, even when they're not sure, to pass on information that worries them. When child abuse is discovered, it's often because a child has told a teacher, or youth worker, or pre-school leader.

Usually, the first person to turn to will be a social worker. Anybody can call their local Social Services offices if there is a child they are worried about, whether it's to do with their job or not. People sometimes call because they are worried about a neighbour's child, or a friend. Sometimes, these calls are from people who have jumped to the wrong conclusion. The child is not at risk at all; they misinterpreted what they saw or heard. Sometimes, hoax calls are made deliberately, to make someone suffer the distress of being accused of child abuse. While both these situations are very difficult for everyone, until the facts are known the social worker has to keep an open mind rather than just assume nothing has happened. Ignoring what seems like a mistaken or malicious report could end up with a dead or seriously injured child.

If a call is made to Social Services, it is considered carefully. Social workers who deal with child abuse are specially trained. Sometimes a social worker enquires into the situation alone, sometimes the enquiry is done jointly with a specially trained police officer. If they think the child is at risk of harm, especially if there might be a criminal court case, the social worker and police officer will work together. If the child and family need help, but it is unlikely that anyone will be prosecuted, the social worker might work without the police (although police will be at the child protection conference, see p61).

The reason that social workers and police officers need to work together is that they have a different job to do. They both need to find out exactly what happened, and they talk to the child together so that the child does not have to go through interview after interview, reliving bad experiences and possibly getting confused by going over and over what happened. But what social workers and police officers do with the information they get is very different.

There are two types of court: criminal (magistrates and crown courts), and civil. The criminal courts deal with all crimes, where it is alleged a law has been broken. The person (or people) accused of breaking that law is called the defendant. They will be asked if they are guilty or not guilty of that crime; it's called 'pleading'. If they plead 'guilty' the court will decide on a punishment. If they plead 'not guilty' there will be a trial. If the court decides, at the end of the trial, that the person is, in fact, guilty, then the criminal court will decide what the punishment will be. When you see a court case in a TV crime drama, it will usually be the criminal court you're watching. Civil courts deal with other matters where there are two opposing sides arguing about an important matter e.g. a divorcing couple arguing about who will have custody of the children.

In a possible child abuse case, the police officer is trying to work out whether or not a crime has been committed. If it has, the police officer will have to gather whatever evidence they can and see if there is enough evidence to prove what happened, and who did what. The police officer works mainly with criminal courts. In this type of court, where people face community punishments or even going to prison, the proof has to be just about certain – allegations must be proved 'beyond reasonable doubt'. When a case goes to trial in the criminal court, if there is any doubt about whether a person has committed a crime, then the person must be found not guilty. Once a verdict has been reached, the police officer is not likely to have any more involvement with the case.

While the police are conducting their enquiries, the social worker needs to make sure the child is safe right now. Will it be safe enough for them to stay at home tonight? If not, is there a relative, or a friend, who can take them in, or will a foster family need to be found in a hurry? And then in the next few weeks, months even, what will happen? What will need to change before home is a safe enough place for the child to go back to? If change doesn't look possible, social workers will have to start looking for a permanent foster or adoptive family. Social workers work mostly in the civil courts, where the level of proof is not so high – cases have to be proved 'on the balance of probabilities'. This means that if child abuse probably happened, it's enough to allow the court to make orders about what will happen to the child. But the civil courts cannot find someone guilty of a criminal offence and punish them; that's the job of the criminal courts.

Very occasionally, the civil court will deal with the aftermath of a criminal trial. For example, if the defendant in a murder trial was found 'not guilty' in the criminal court, they could still possible be sued for compensation ('damages') by the family of the murdered person. This would happen in the civil court. Since the level of proof is lower ('on the balance of probabilities' rather than 'beyond reasonable doubt'), you may well have a case where a criminal court says someone is innocent but the civil court finds that they did the crime. Strange, but true.

The child protection conference (see p.60) can still happen whether there is to be a criminal court case, a civil court case or simply some work done by a social worker with the family. Whatever is done, it has to be agreed that it will be the best thing for the child. The child's safety and welfare is always the top priority. Unlike the police, it is quite common for a social worker to still be working with the family a long time after court cases have been decided.

The Child Protection Register

Every area of the country is required by law to keep a child protection register. This is a list of children, 0-18 years, who are considered to be at such a strong risk of abuse that they and their families need special attention from a social worker and maybe other professionals too. Before any decision is made, there will be a meeting, usually called a child protection conference. At the meeting there will be a mixture of people who know the child well and some who are there because they have a lot of experience and skill in child protection, although they don't necessarily know the child. The child's parents are usually invited to the conference. Sometimes the child is also invited for at least part of it, if they are old enough to understand what is going on and want to be there. If not, the social worker will talk to the child to make sure the people at the conference know how the child feels and what they want to happen. If there is more than one child in the family, the conference will talk about all the children in the same way.

At the conference there will be a group of people who work with children – for example, nurses, teachers, social workers and others. Some of them will be people who know the child and family. If the child is at school, a teacher from the school will be invited. If the child is very young the Health Visitor is invited – and so on. The point of the meeting is to get people together who can help to keep the child safe and help the family get its life back on track.

The Chair of the meeting will be a senior social worker. There will be a report on what has happened, why the meeting has been called. Then the various people who have dealt with the child and the family tell the meeting what they know about them. They will talk about the good things going on in the child's life as well as the difficult things. Once all the information that people have has been shared, it's time for the people there to say what they think should be done. The first big decision is whether or not the child or children's name(s) should go on the child protection register. If there is more than one child in the family, each child will be dealt with separately. So it's possible that one child can be on the register but a brother or sister is not.

For each child, the people at the conference will be asked, Has this child suffered, or are they likely to suffer, significant harm? (We looked at what significant harm is on p.4) Every person there is asked to say what they think about this. Hopefully, everyone will feel the same way, but if people can't agree the Chair has to make the final decision. If the child's name is going on to the register, it will go on under one or more of the four categories that we looked at earlier in the book: neglect, physical abuse, sexual abuse or emotional abuse.

If the child is going to be placed on the register, a 'core group' is formed at that meeting to work with the family and the child. As soon as a child is on the register, people start working to try and get them off again. The core group will consist of a social worker and some of the people who work with the child and/or the family regularly; these are the people who will try and keep the child safe by helping to make whatever changes are needed. They will make a plan together and work out who will do what. For example, a health visitor might agree to visit more often to support a mother who isn't coping with a baby. The school might assign a teacher the child knows well to keep a special eye on them, and to make times for the parents to come in and talk. A youth worker who knows the child well might agree to set aside some time to talk to them and be a listening ear whenever they need it. Maybe a nursery place will be made available to give Mum a much-needed break. There are all sorts of things that might be happening, and exactly what is offered will depend on each individual case.

More often than not, the child will still live at home while all this goes on; if not with their own family, then with a relative, perhaps, or in a foster family. But nobody wants to take a child away from their parents unless the risks are so high that there's no other way to keep the child safe.

After a time, perhaps three or six months, the people who came to the first child protection conference are invited back to another meeting, called the child protection review. They will look at what has been going on since the first meeting and then make the decision again; should the child's name be kept on the register, or have things changed enough to make people feel the child is safe again? If the child stays on, the plan will be modified, or maybe a new one made, and the core group starts again.

If the child's name comes off the register, it doesn't mean there's no help on offer any more. Social workers might well carry on supporting a family for some time, to make sure things don't go wrong again.

Preventing Child Abuse

Parents who abuse their children often do it because they're stressed out and at the end of their tether. They suddenly snap and lash out, physically and mentally. It's important to know what stresses you out, to recognise when it is happening, and to have some kind of way of dealing with it. Most people come into close contact with children at some stage of their lives, as parents, step-parents, uncles, aunts, babysitters and so on. So it's a good idea to be prepared, and get some practice in!

○ Try to make a list of the top ten needs a child must have fulfilled if they are going to grow up happy and secure and able to make relationships later in life. To make it a bit more difficult, you cannot use 'love' as one of them. Everyone would accept that children need love, but how should that love show itself? For example, how important is it to praise your child? Or give your child security? Nor can you use the word 'home'. It is a word that means a lot more than having a roof over your head – what are the important things that make a place 'home'?

○ Discuss this: if you become a parent, what do you think will be the most likely causes of stress for you? For example, if you are somebody who needs a lot of sleep, it might be the sleepless nights that often come with a baby. If you like to go out most evenings, it might be the feeling of being cooped up. Think of as many possible causes of stress for parents as you can.

○ How do you cope now, when you're stressed out with your life? Would that work if you were a parent? How would you cope with the build-up of stress that almost every parent experiences, without harming your child? Share strategies for dealing with stress with the people in your small group.

○ Incorporate the best ideas into a poster or leaflet for use in baby clinics or GP surgeries. Try to make it eye-catching with an attention-seeking headline or illustrations or graphics. Include the number of the NSPCC helpline for parents (Parentline Plus: 0808 800 2222)

If you are pleased with the result, why not ask your local GP surgery if they would like to use it?

Telephone Numbers and Websites

NSPCC helpline (24 hours)   0808 800 5000
www.nspcc.org.uk

Childline (24 hours)   0800 1111
www.childline.org.uk

Samaritans (24 hours)   0345 909090
www.samaritans.org.uk

British Association for Counselling and Psychotherapy
www.bacp.co.uk

Get Connected   0808 808 4994
Free, confidential advice, whatever the problem

Sexwise   0800 282930
Free, confidential advice on sex, contraception and relationships

MindinfoLine   0845 7660163
(for help dealing with   (daytime Mon – Fri)
mental illness)
www.mentalhealthcare.org.uk

National Domestic Violence   0808 2000 247
Freephone helpline (24 hours)
www.refuge.org.uk

National Alcohol Helpline   0800 9178282
(24 hours)
www.alanon.org/alateen.html

National Drugs helpline   0800 776600
(24 hours)
www.coaf.org

Net Smart Rules

Keep the peace! Always check that your parent/carer is happy for you to enter a chatroom.

Don't dish it out! When you visit a chatroom, it is a good idea to sign on using a nickname, and when you're chatting don't give out your real name, your email address, your age, your phone number, where you live, your school, whether you are a boy or girl, and don't publish or send out a picture of yourself.

It is best to keep all this info to yourself because you never know who might be in there and can see it.

Signing up! It's not always straightforward!

Often before you can join a chatroom in the first place, or get a new email address, buy something or do other things on the internet, you will need to sign up online and give out some personal info like your name, address and telephone number.

Before you do this, first ask your parent/carer if that is OK. Then check how the company providing the service is planning to use the information you give them. Will all or some of it appear online as part of a profile that anyone can see when you use the service, or can you choose not to allow that? If you can, do.

Some chatrooms will insist on publishing some details about you every time you go online. They may just take bits of the profile you have already given them when you signed up.

Others will allow you to create a new profile specially for publication on the internet. Either way these profiles can generally be viewed by anyone using the same chatroom or service. So stick to your nickname, or just don't fill it in! This way there's less chance of people contacting you when you might not want them to.

Unless you tell them not to, some companies might pass all or some of this information on to other companies and then you could get bombarded with spam (unwanted emails). Check any forms you fill in - most have a small box you can tick or un-tick to make sure your information is not passed on.

Wise up! You can't always be sure it's only people your age in a chatroom. Chat safely: it could be an adult winding you up or trying to trick you.

Pop ya collar! Leave a chatroom the moment anything worries you. Let your parent/carer know what's up and report it to the chat service provider. Save any conversations that you think could prove someone has been bullying or harassing you. Some chatrooms have instructions on how to do this or you can look at the directions on www.fkbko.co.uk

Web-wasters! Report bad-taste and bad-attitude messages in chatrooms to your parent/carer and your internet service provider or whoever runs the chatroom.

Back up! Never arrange to meet anyone in the real world who you only know online, unless your parent/carer agrees and comes with you. If your parent/carer does agree and comes with you, never arrange to meet at your online friend's house. Stay in a public place like a café or shopping centre: it's safer.

It's everywhere! The internet is no longer something you only use through your computer at school or at home. Some mobile phones provide internet access, some games consoles do as well. You need to stay just as sussed when on the internet via phones or consoles, as with a computer.

Reality check! Keep clear of over 18 chatrooms, websites and other parts of the internet intended for adults. The warnings are for your protection and adult sites can sometimes do serious damage to your phone bill.

Word up! All passwords you use on computers are PRIVATE. Keep them to yourself.

Attack of the attached! Viruses can spread through email attachments, causing serious damage or even destroy your computer. Make sure the emails are from people you know and trust before opening them. Even this isn't always foolproof so if you're unsure - scan it for viruses first or bin it!

Ask your internet service provider if it automatically screens emails for viruses, or try and choose a web-based e-mail account that does this automatically, or at least offers you the option to scan them. Always have a virus-checker onboard anyway. See www.norton.com and www.mcafee.com to find out more.

Have fun and stay Net Smart!

Published: Monday, 22 November, 2004 08:12
Last updated: Wednesday, 2 November, 2005 12:23
About NCH | Privacy policy
Registered charity no.1097940/company no.4764232

A Final Note

This book has looked at a whole variety of things that can go wrong in families. But remember that for most people, the family is a great thing to be a part of. Every family goes through bad times, but this doesn't mean they abuse their children. Most children are happy, secure, well loved and well cared for. And if we all do whatever it is we can do to stop child abuse, we are helping to build the kind of world where books like this will have no use.